BERMUDA

BERMUDA

Roger A. Bruns and Haldon K. Richardson

CHELSEA HOUSE

Copyright © 1986 by Chelsea House Publishers, 5014 West Chester Pike, Edgemont, Pa. 19028. All rights reserved.
   Reproduction in whole or part by any means whatsoever
   without permission of the publisher is prohibited by law.
Printed in the United States of America.

LV6-005086

Library of Congress Cataloging-in-Publication Data

Bruns, Roger.
   Bermuda.
   Includes index.
   Summary: An introduction to the history, topography, economy, politics, industry, people, and culture of Bermuda.

1. Bermuda Islands.   [1. Bermuda Islands]
I. Richardson, Haldon K.   II. Title.   III. Series.
FI631.2.B78   1986   972.99   86-11689

ISBN 1-55546-159-X

Editorial Director: Susan R. Williams
Senior Editor: Rebecca Stefoff
Associate Editor: Rafaela Ellis
Art Director: Maureen McCafferty
Series Designer: Anita Noble
Project Coordinator: Kathleen P. Luczak

ACKNOWLEDGEMENTS

The authors and publishers are grateful to the Bermuda Department of Tourism for photographs and information.

Contents

Map 6
From Shipwrecks to Tourist Paradise 8
The Land 30
The Parishes 36
The People and Society 51
Of Many Faiths 69
Government: In the British Image 77
A Sports Lover's Haven 81
A Tourist Economy 87
Index 93

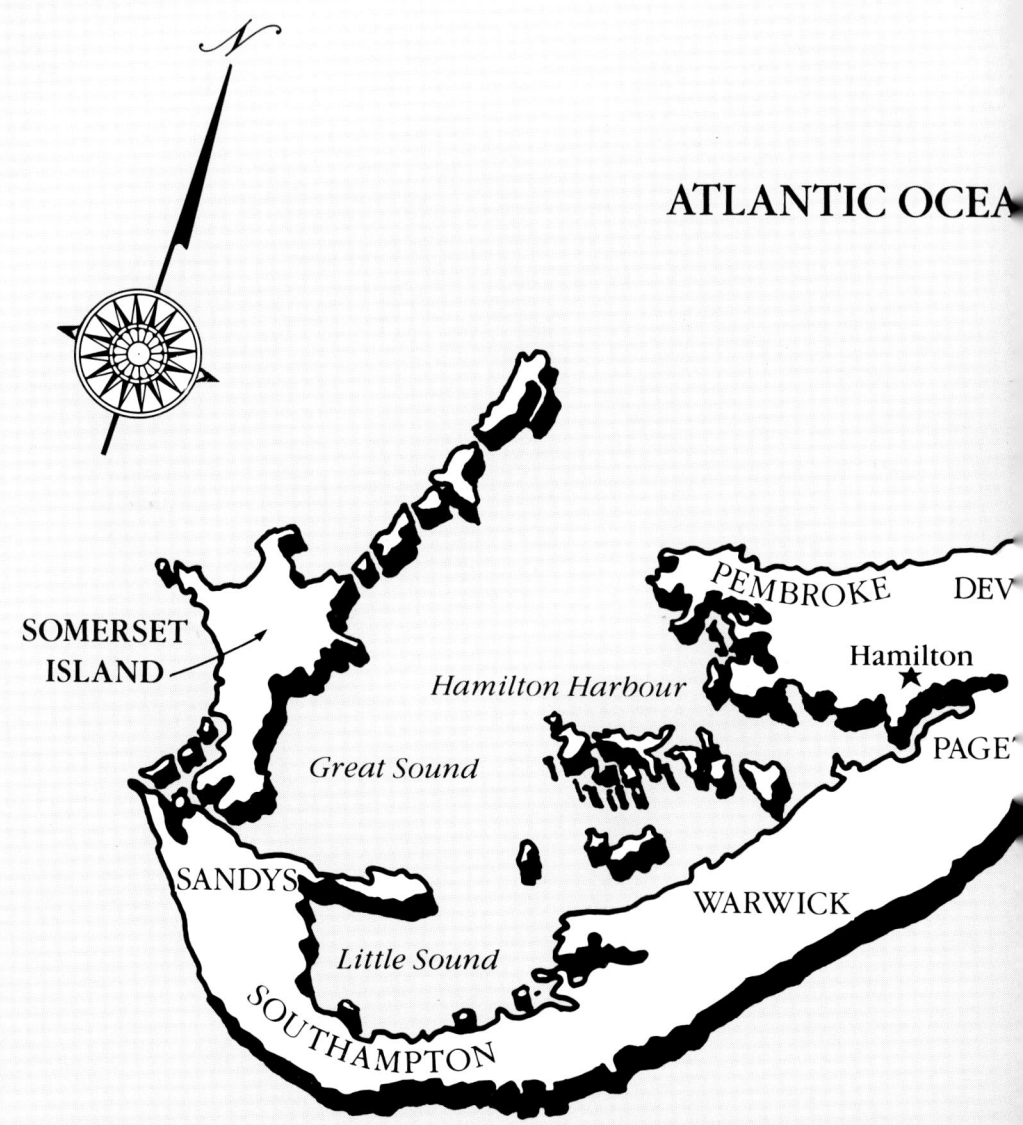

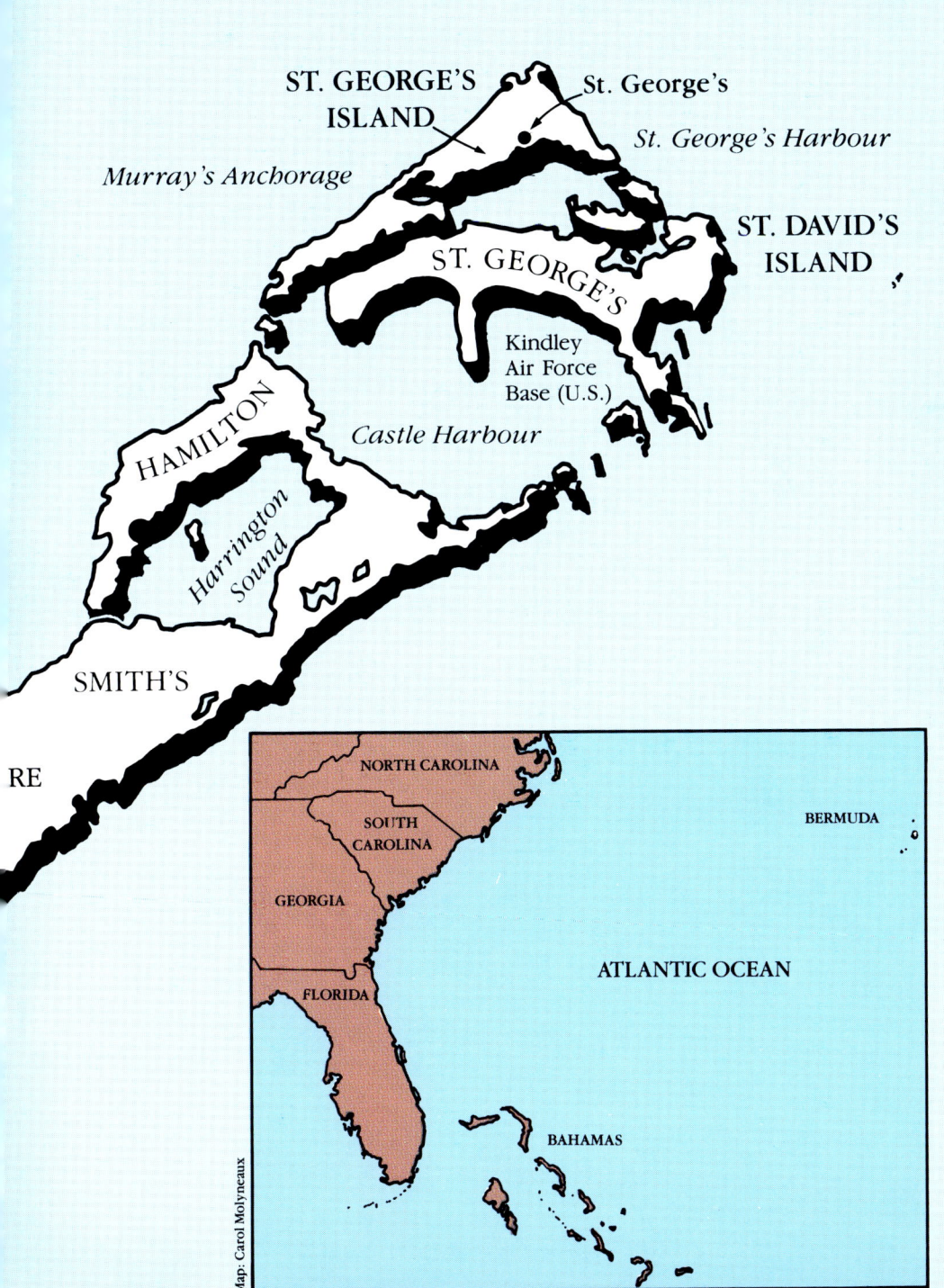

From Shipwrecks to a Tourist Paradise

The island chain of Bermuda lies in the western Atlantic, about 650 miles (1,040 kilometers) southeast of Cape Hatteras, North Carolina, and about 3,300 miles (5,280 kilometers) southwest of London, England. Sixteenth-century mariners told tales of horror and mystery about Bermuda, which they called the "Isle of Devils." They dreaded its howling winds; they told of swirling seas, hazardous coral reefs, and hundreds of ships that, venturing too close, had been violently swallowed in the Bermuda

An old Dutch drawing shows survivors of the wreck of the Sea Venture

waters. They talked of water demons, of blue ghosts, of the eerie cries of the cahow birds—cries that made the skin crawl with dread—of the fearful storms, roaring as if they were tumults from the Devil himself. Even William Shakespeare mentioned, in his play *The Tempest,* the "still-vex'd Bermooths."

Scores of vessels today lie on the ocean floor, telling the grim story of the sailors who fought those water demons and lost. But the story of Bermuda is also the story of those who survived and found there not a place of horror but a bountiful island.

In 1609, James I sat on the throne of England. It was a time of seafaring exploration, when Britain challenged Spain for control of the seas and the new lands discovered in America. A small British settlement called Jamestown, near the Chesapeake Bay, had barely survived two bitter winters. Determined to maintain its new colony in North America, Britain sent food, supplies, and new settlers to Jamestown.

In May of 1609, the ship *Sea Venture,* a three-thousand-ton, full-rigged flagship, joined a supply fleet bound from England to America. Commanded by Captain Christopher Newport, a one-armed sailor who had made an earlier voyage to America, and Sir George Somers, the Admiral of the fleet, the ship carried 150 men, women, and children, including the newly appointed lieutenant governor of Virginia, Sir Thomas Gates. The passengers on board the *Sea Venture* had been entrusted by the King with the task of building a thriving colony in Virginia.

Sir George Somers drew this map of the Bermudas in 1609

Eight days from landfall on the Virginia coast, the *Sea Venture* was beset by the choppy waves and roaring winds that had taken many a ship to the ocean floor. Rocked and jolted by the treacherous storm, the *Sea Venture* soon disappeared from the view of the other ships in the fleet. Weeks passed, then months, and no word was heard in America or London of the fate of the *Sea Venture*.

It was assumed that the ship and its passengers had been tragically lost.

They had not. For two days after the storm hit, the ship had floundered. The fury of the winds had been, as one crew member later described it, "like a hell of darkness turned black upon us." With the ship slowly taking on water and breaking apart in the driving wind and violent sea, Admiral Somers spotted land. Through treacherous shoals and outcroppings of dark coral, the *Sea Venture* rocked and swayed, finally crashing

A map published in 1635 shows the Sea Venture on the reef

11

between huge rocks. The ship had ruptured—but it had made land. The passengers rowed ashore in longboats. They had landed on the dreaded "Isle of Devils."

What they found, however, were peaceful islands, fine bays, and a rich assortment of wildflowers, fruits, and trees, especially cedars and palmettos. Here also were fish, crabs, and oysters in massive numbers. In the first book published in England about the wreck of the *Sea Venture,* Silvanus Jordan said fish were so abundant that men were reluctant to step into the waters for fear of being bitten. The stranded passengers and crew found wild hogs, huge tortoises (each large enough to feed 20 people), and duck, teal and other seabirds that laid enormous eggs. The "Isle of Devils" had turned out to be an island paradise.

During the next ten months, the Somers group built two small vessels to continue their voyage to Virginia. But Somers and his people had quickly seen the potential for future colonization in Bermuda. They saw that its plentiful natural resources could make this land valuable to British interests. Three men from the *Sea Venture* were left to live in Bermuda until other settlers and supplies could be sent.

Colonization and Early History

In July of 1612, 60 settlers under the command of Richard Moore arrived in Bermuda in the vessel *Plough.* The colonization of the island had begun. The newcomers found that the three men who had been left behind by Somers in 1610 were

The State House, Bermuda's oldest building, was built in 1619; the mortar used in its construction was made of turtle oil and lime

The shipwrecked settlers found a paradise, not an "Isle of Devils"

thriving on their island. Britain claimed Bermuda, and Moore became the islands' first governor. Since the wreck of the *Sea Venture* more than three and a half centuries ago, the isles of Bermuda have been continuously inhabited by the British.

The British, however, were probably not the first discoverers of Bermuda. According to most historians, the Spanish navigator Juan de Bermudez saw the islands in the early 1500s. Although it is unlikely that he actually landed there, a map published in 1511 shows an island called "La Bermuda," obviously named after the Spaniard. Other navigators, including at least one Englishman, apparently visited the islands in the 16th century. But the *Sea Venture* paved the way for colonization. The recorded history of Bermuda begins with George Somers and his people. These early settlers honored their leader by naming the major town St. George's. Founded eight years before the Pilgrims landed at Plymouth Rock, St. George's was the capital of the islands for more than 200 years. Located at the northeast end of Bermuda, it is one of the oldest English-speaking communities in the Western Hemisphere.

By 1616, the Bermuda Company had received a charter from the king to establish the colony and had divided it into

Gates Fort was built to repel an invasion that never arrived

eight large parishes (similar to counties in the United States). Bermuda's first parliament was held in 1620 in St. Peter's Church. Soon, a State House was built. A ninth parish, St. George's, was created in the latter part of the 17th century and Bermuda officially became a British Crown Colony governed by the monarch.

The British built several forts in Bermuda to protect the islands and channels from invaders. Gates Fort in St. George's dates from 1615. A huge fort named St. Catherine was later built in St. George's, near where Admiral Somers first came ashore. The fortifications were never needed; the invasion never came.

Slaves—blacks from the West Indies and Indians from English colonies in North America—were first brought to Bermuda in the early 1600s. Although Bermuda needed fewer slaves than the cotton fields of the American South or the sugar cane plantations of the West Indies, many slaves were used as servants and laborers. And in many cases their treatment was especially cruel. Slaves were sometimes beaten, underfed, separated from their families, and bought and sold like cattle. In the 17th and 18th centuries, Bermuda was the scene of several slave revolts (as were some other British colonies). The revolts led only to even more repressive treatment.

Because of its economic unprofitability and because of the reform efforts of political and religious leaders, the slave system gradually eroded in Bermuda. In 1834, slavery was officially abolished in the British Empire, including Bermuda. Many black Bermudians today are descendants of the freed slaves.

After the 17th century, whaling was important to Bermuda's economy

An 1890 photograph shows the cedars used in shipbuilding

The witch dunkings of the 1600s are reenacted for today's tourists

The 17th century was a time of vigorous building in Bermuda. In the 1620s, Bermudians built bridges connecting the main islands. Churches and other structures were also built. Bermuda created its first coins at this time. One side of the coin showed a hog, in honor of the wild hogs that had provided food for the first shipwrecked colonists. These copper coins became known as "Hog Money."

Bermuda, like England and the North American colonies, conducted witch hunts in the 17th century. Men and women suspected of witchcraft were manacled to the stake and burned

18

to death on flimsy "evidence" that they were agents of the Devil. One man was killed for allegedly bewitching another man's turkeys. Suspected witches were sometimes bound hand and foot and thrown into water; if they floated, they were hanged as witches. Fortunately, the mass religious hysteria of the witch hunts disappeared from the islands almost as suddenly as it had arrived.

Bermudians quickly discovered one special natural resource that became vital to their growth: cedar. This tough and close-grained tree could be used to build sailing vessels. The Bermudians made their principal livelihood as maritime traders, developing routes to all parts of the East Coast of North America and the Caribbean Sea.

The islanders also began using special ships to catch whales. For a long time, whaling was an important economic enterprise; six whaling stations were located in the islands.

By the end of the 17th century, Bermuda's maritime commerce had begun to make the islands stable and prominent among the world's seafarers. Traders voyaged to the Turks Islands in the Bahamas for salt and bartered for West Indian rum and African slaves. They also carried food to the American colonies and to Nova Scotia. In the 17th century, Americans raved about Bermuda's oranges, and travelers to Bermuda claimed they could smell orange blossoms as far as 30 miles (48 kilometers) from shore.

Of all the enterprises of the early Bermudians, one in particular was the most profitable—although the most violent.

Many Bermudians became pirates. Because the islands lay in the middle of major trading lanes, some of Bermuda's more robust adventurers roamed the seas in search of spoils. A story is still told about Captain Darrell Harvey, privateer extraordinaire, who set sail with a crew of 125—far more than necessary to man his ship. It was obvious that Captain Harvey had something far different in mind. A few months later Harvey returned to Bermuda with 18 ships, all captured on the open seas and manned by members of his original crew.

Some ingenious Bermudians found a way to capture unsuspecting ships without even leaving the islands. They rearranged beacons in the surrounding waters to lure ships onto reefs and rocks. They waited for the inevitable doom that lay in store for

Buildings are made of limestone quarried on the islands

the ships and then plundered their cargoes. Some Bermudian storytellers now contend that virtually everyone in those days was a pirate. Legend says a man once burst excitedly into a church service and screamed, "There's a ship approaching the reef!" The annoyed minister, so the story goes, spoke to the congregation: "Everyone here will remain in their pews until I take off my robe . . . then we'll all have a fair head start."

The doom of the victims was the profit of the privateers. The money chests of St. George's were soon filled with foreign coins and goods looted by pirates. During the boom years of such piracy, some of Bermuda's most stylish homes appeared, many of them built from yet another of the island's many natural resources—limestone, which lies under much of Bermuda's topsoil. Cut from hillside quarries, the soft and porous stone was easily hewn into building blocks.

During the American Revolution, Bermudians were bitterly divided between loyalty to Britain, their mother country, and America, their principal trading partner. By the mid-18th century, Bermuda had become dependent on the American colonies for food. The islanders faced possible starvation if their trading ships were prevented by the British from doing business in America.

In 1775, General George Washington persuaded some citizens of Bermuda to secure gunpowder for his troops in exchange for food. One sultry August night, a band of islanders stealthily removed virtually all of the colony's powder and rowed it out to two American warships waiting beyond the

Whitecaps mark the treacherous reef that encircles the islands

reefs. The Bermudians did not go hungry during the American Revolution.

By 1815, business and commercial activity had grown substantially in the central and western areas of Bermuda. The country's leaders decided to transfer the seat of government from St. George's to Hamilton, a bustling settlement near the center of the islands. Bermuda now had two important cities: the beloved St. George's and the new colonial capital, Hamilton.

Among the immigrants who made the long voyage from Europe to North America in the 17th century were Portuguese settlers, who began to arrive in Bermuda in the 1840s. To increase the islands' workforce, the Bermudian government encouraged Portuguese immigration. Although they were confined mostly to agricultural work in the early years in the islands, the Portuguese are today an integral part of Bermudian society.

During the American Civil War, most islanders' sympathies were with the Confederacy. Although Bermuda was officially neutral (as it had been during the American Revolution), the islands nevertheless traded with the South. St. George's harbor was wild with activity. Paddle-wheel boats such as the *R.E. Lee* did a thriv-

Today a peaceful yacht basin, Hamilton Harbour was once the home port of pirates and smugglers

ing business with the Confederates. The North had attempted to blockade ships from reaching Southern ports, but the experienced Bermudian sea veterans easily outwitted their Northern pursuers.

Blockade running was profitable business. Captains willing to take on the challenge made as much as $5,000 for each round trip from Bermuda to North Carolina. The South traded cotton for arms and other equipment that the islanders procured from British ships. For a time, St. George's warehouses bulged with goods for the war effort, but soon it was all over. Today, the paddle-wheeler *Mary Celestia* lies rusting off Bermuda's south coast, where she was ripped apart after striking a reef. She sank with a cargo of munitions and bacon that had been destined for Dixie.

During the Civil War, Joseph Hayne Rainey, a black slave from South Carolina, set himself up as a barber in St. George's. When Rainey returned to his native state after the war, he was elected to the United States Congress.

During the last quarter of the 19th century, the islands exported many vegetable products, especially onions. So brisk

was the trade in onions to New York markets that Hamilton was for a time called "Onion Town." But the onion market collapsed when United States farmers discovered how to grow the vegetable themselves. To help its own farmers, the United States began to levy high taxes on imported vegetable goods. These taxes put Bermuda out of the export farming business.

The Growth of a New Industry

But the industry that would sustain Bermuda to this day had already gained a foothold on the islands. In the late 19th century, with the beginning of steamship services, the tourist industry began to flourish. Mark Twain once remarked that Americans "on their way to heaven call at Bermuda and think they've arrived." Bermudians now began to take advantage of their land's spectacular natural beauty and climate. From piracy to blockade-running to food products, Bermudians had experimented with industries; they found an enduring source of income in tourism.

The tourist industry slowly grew, attracting people who

The **Robert E. Lee** *was one of the paddle-wheelers that traded with the Confederates during the Civil War*

wanted to escape harsh Northern winters. The face of Bermuda began to change, as hotels began to dot the beaches and towns and tourists from America and Europe sauntered along admiring the islands' natural wonders. At the turn of the century, United States President Woodrow Wilson frequently visited Bermuda. He once signed a petition asking the Bermuda legislature to ban automobiles from the islands—a plea that was heeded for almost 40 years. Wilson wanted the beauty of Bermuda to remain unspoiled by the newfangled machines.

World War I brought hardship to Bermuda as well as to almost every other part of the world. Shipping was crippled, and food and supplies became scarce. Fishermen stayed close to shore,

Bermudian streets owe their colorful tropical appearance to the pastel washes used on the limestone buildings

In 1973, racial turmoil led to the assassination of the governor and his aide in these gardens at Government House

fearful of German warships. Many Bermudians guarded the fortress of the British Navy on the islands, and the Bermuda Volunteer Rifle Corps served in battle in France.

Later, during the "Roaring Twenties" in the United States, when liquor was prohibited, Bermuda became especially popular with upper-class tourists, who could drink on steamships and in the new hotels that quickly filled up with new guests. The era of Prohibition in the United States was an era of boom in Bermuda.

Soon, the first commercial passenger airline flights between

New York City and Bermuda began. Along with several steamships that operated weekly, the airlines made access to the islands easier than it had ever been.

True to its ancient reputation as a land of mystery, Bermuda during World War II was the scene of plots, secret diplomacy, and intricate intelligence operations. In the cellars of the famous pink Princess Hotel in Hamilton, British code experts deciphered microdot messages sent by German spies. The messages were intercepted in mail carried on the New York-Europe route aboard planes that landed in Bermuda to refuel. Bermudians also tracked enemy U-boats. On one occasion, they even saved a collection of paintings stolen by the Nazis in France. The Impressionist works were taken off a ship in Bermuda, hidden in a bank vault during the war, and later returned to their startled but grateful owner.

From the islands, the British Royal Navy patrolled the Atlantic. With German submarines menacing North American shipping during the war, Great Britain asked Bermuda to give land for the establishment of United States naval and military bases. The United States built an airfield that is used by Bermudians today.

Bermuda also became the meeting site of such political notables as Winston Churchill, Dwight Eisenhower, and British Prime Minister Harold Macmillan. In later years, John F. Kennedy, Richard Nixon, and Prime Minister Edward Heath also held summit meetings in Bermuda.

In the 1960s Bermuda, much like the United States, was racked by growing racial tensions (the majority of Bermuda's residents are black). Blacks protested against discrimination in education, housing, and jobs. Black leaders pointed out that almost no blacks were executives in the hotel industry and that they were not fairly represented in government.

In 1963, the Progressive Labour Party, Bermuda's first political party, began to agitate on behalf of nonwhite citizens. In 1968, the year that the great American black leader, Martin Luther King, Jr., was assassinated in the United States, a minor scuffle in Hamilton turned into a race riot. And in the spring of 1973, political troubles increased sharply. Bermuda's governor, Sir Richard Sharples, and his aide were assassinated while taking an evening stroll in the grounds of Government House. Several months later, following the hanging of the convicted assassins, more riots erupted in the black communities, causing millions of dollars in destruction and leading to strict curfew hours.

Racial turmoil in Bermuda has led to serious demands for national independence from Britain. Political unrest and rioting in 1977 prompted government efforts to end racial discrimination and to begin independence talks. Although those talks were later called off, the question of independence is still important for many Bermudians.

Since 1615 the motto of Bermuda has been "Quo Fata Ferunt," which means "Whither the Fates will carry us." From the days of seafaring adventurers to the modern tourist paradise, the islands have had a colorful history. Bermuda remains a fascinating land of almost magical beauty, an ocean haven of turbulent waters with a turbulent past. As Mark Twain once said in Bermuda: "You go to heaven if you want, I'll stay right here."

The Land

One hundred million years ago, a tremendous volcano erupted at the bottom of the Atlantic Ocean. For years its lava poured into the sea, forming a huge undersea mountain range. Some of these mountains rose 15,000 feet (4,950 meters) and broke the surface of the water.

The volcanic rock of the craggy coastline was created millions of years ago in an undersea eruption

Lush plant life is abundant, although the topsoil is thin

Bermuda is a part of a group of more than 150 such volcanic islands, 20 of which are inhabited. Seen from the air, the islands look like a huge fishhook. Twenty-two miles (35 kilometers) long, Bermuda is less than two miles (three kilometers) wide at its widest point. Its area is only 21 square miles (57 square kilometers). The islands, protected by coral reefs that have grown around them and prevent the sea from eroding them, contain rolling, lush green hills. Jagged promontories of volcanic rock break up the coast, separating the beaches into soft pockets of rose-colored sand. For countless centuries the relentless tide and the whipping winds have carved the land, hollowing out natural arches and sculpting towers and peaks at the ocean's edge.

Although animal and plant life is abundant, the soil on Bermuda is very thin. In many cases, all that was needed to make a "paved" road was to scrape off the thin layer of soil and expose the limestone (called Bermuda coral) beneath. All of the buildings on the islands are made of this stone.

Bermuda's weather, although mild, is unpredictable. Its mid-Atlantic location exposes it to winds and storms. The subtropical climate owes its consistent warmth to the Gulf Stream, a warm current that flows north and west of the islands.

Divers explore the coral reef, rich in plant and animal life

Spring comes to Bermuda in November and lasts through mid-April, when the temperature ranges from 60 to 70 degrees Fahrenheit (16 to 21 degrees Centigrade). Fall and winter are, for all practical purposes, non-existent. Throughout the year, evening temperatures are usually several degrees cooler than daytime. Because of the reef, the waters around Bermuda are clear and warm and have a turquoise color. The temperature of the water ranges from 62 degrees Fahrenheit (17 degrees Centigrade) in spring to 80 degrees F (27 degrees C) in summer.

Over the centuries, the wind and waves have carved colossal natural arches in the coastal rocks

The Coral Reef

Bermuda is a cluster of unusually shaped islands of various sizes, called an archipelago. Around these beautiful isles is a living, growing coral reef.

A coral reef the size of Bermuda's requires thousands of years to grow. It begins with one tiny plant and one tiny animal. Kept warm by the waters of the Gulf Stream, the animal gets nourishment from the plant. The plant, in turn, depends upon the animal for survival. This relationship, where each is dependent upon the other, is called symbiosis.

The reef is majestic and inspiring. As a snorkeler or diver swims along the reef, he realizes how small and vulnerable humans are compared with life in the sea. The reef also demonstrates the beauty, diversity, and unity of life in natural environments.

But the reef can cause drastic problems for ships. Since the discovery of the islands by Juan de Bermudez, more than 120 ships—sailing under the flags of many nations—are known to have met their ends on the reef. As the coral has grown nearer to the surface of the water, it has formed an oval around the islands, broken only by shallow, almost unnavigable channels. Most of the ships that have sunk have gone down on the reef north and west of Bermuda.

Treasures of untold worth remain to be salvaged from these sunken ships; priceless gems, gold, and silver have already been recovered. Many of the wrecks are Spanish treasure galleons, full of booty from Mexico, the West Indies, and South America. The excavation of sunken treasure is risky, costly, and time-consuming, but it has paid handsomely to the few who have the temperament and perseverance to pursue it.

Priceless treasures of gold and jewels, salvaged from the sea bottom, are housed in the Maritime Museum

The Parishes

Distinct differences in natural features and human settlement occur throughout the islands of the Bermuda "fishhook." A closer look at each of Bermuda's nine parishes reveals the geographical characteristics of the islands from west to east.

Sandys Parish

Located in the westernmost part of the islands, Sandys Parish is lush with foliage: flowering hibiscus lines the roads and paths. The parish includes the southwestern tip of the main island and the smaller islands of Somerset, Boaz, and Ireland North and

Horseshoe Bay, Southampton Parish, has beautiful beaches

Riddell's Bay, between Southampton and Warwick Parishes

South. The main island is connected to the rest of the parish by the Watford Bridge at Sugar Cane Point.

Sandys is bordered with expansive beaches and contains two beautiful harbors, two nature reserves, and dozens of bays and coves. The gentle tranquility of these snug harbors and coves and the coziness of the flower-lined roads add charm to this sparsely populated parish.

Southampton Parish

Southeast of Sandys Parish is the most breathtakingly beautiful area of the entire island chain. Long and narrow, Southampton Parish contains magnificent beaches and crystal-clear bays, such as Stonehole, Church, and Horseshoe Bays. Just off one of Southampton's beaches is a six-mile (nine-kilometer) stretch known as "The Boilers." Here the reef has grown almost to the water's surface, causing the surf to churn constantly.

Much of the land is hilly. The most notable rise is Gibbs Hill, 245 feet (73 meters) above sea level. The Gibbs Hill lighthouse ascends an additional 117 feet (35 meters) from the top of the hill. A perfect vantage point from which to observe the islands, the lighthouse is visible to ships 40 miles (64 kilometers) out at sea.

Warwick Parish

Most of the parishes of Bermuda were named after members of the original settling company of 1610. Warwick was named after the Second Earl of Warwick.

The grand beaches of Southampton continue in Warwick Parish; the south shore of Warwick has Jobson's Cove and Warwick Long Bay, where breathtaking cliffs rise sharply from the beach. The surf is higher than that of Southampton's south shore.

This parish also contains Warwick Camp, a military installation used by British soldiers during both World Wars. It is now used by the Bermudian volunteer soldiers.

Paget Parish

Because the city of Hamilton is nearby, more people live in Paget Parish than in the parishes farther west.

The greatest expanses of unspoiled land found in this part of Bermuda are the 36-acre Botanical Garden and the 26-acre Paget Marsh. The marsh is the only place in Bermuda where the forest has remained untouched since the first settlers arrived. It contains palmetto trees, cedar trees, and a mangrove swamp.

Paget also contains Grape Bay, Hamilton Harbour, and Hungry Bay. The latter is one of the islands' most extensive fish-feeding areas.

Pembroke Parish

Located in the center of the island chain, Pembroke Parish is a peninsula. Here Bermuda's capital city, Hamilton, is found. The

Motorbikes carry sunbathers and bikers to the islands' most remote beaches and forests

end of the peninsula, north of busy Hamilton Harbour, is barren. Craggy rocks reach into the sea. Just off these rocks is a small speck of land called Cobbler's Island. During the 18th and 19th centuries, the bodies of slaves who had been murdered by their owners were exhibited on Cobbler's Island to discourage other blacks from trying to gain freedom.

Founded in 1790, Hamilton is the present capital of Bermuda. Hamilton's City Hall, located on Church Street, is the center of the island's theatrical and musical activities. Also on Church Street is Bermuda's Cathedral of the Most Holy Trinity. The church, made almost entirely of Bermuda limestone, was built in 1894.

The Sessions House, where the island's governing body meets, is on Parliament Street. In front of the Sessions House sits the Cabinet Building, also built of limestone. The governor presides over Parliament here each October.

A wedding in Hamilton is complete with traditional horse-drawn carriages

East of downtown Hamilton, Happy Valley Road climbs to Fort Hamilton. Built by the Duke of Wellington (who defeated Napoleon at Waterloo), the old fort has a moat—now dry and filled with flowers. Although today its upper level is grassy and scattered with park benches, the fort stands as a constant reminder to Bermudians of a more warlike day gone by.

Devonshire Parish

Located just east of Paget and Pembroke Parishes is Devonshire Parish, the greenest and hilliest area of the islands. The Devonshire Marsh is found here. The water of the parish is high in salt content; before enough wells had been dug and water distilleries built, the parish's water was brackish.

Verdmont Historic House in Hamilton displays furniture made of native cedar; it also features the deep fireplace, which can be opened from outside, that is characteristic of Bermudian architecture

British pageantry is part of Bermudian life; here, an honor guard prepares to raise the flag in front of the Cabinet Building

Devonshire's northern coast is lined with jagged, rocky cliffs. The southern shore of this sparsely populated parish is much gentler, with a few small colonies and private beaches. The southern edge of Devonshire consists of rock formations that show all the stages of geologic development since the islands were formed one hundred million years ago.

Smith's Parish

Smith's Parish is bordered by Harrington Sound on the northeast and the Atlantic on the north and south. It contains two bird sanctuaries and the small town of Flatts Village. Two centuries ago, Flatts Village was a stopover for smugglers before they went through customs at St. George's.

The winding road around Harrington Sound is thick with oleander, a poisonous evergreen shrub with prominent red or white flowers. Next to the road is Devil's Hole Pond, full of a wide variety of fish and turtles.

Hamilton's City Hall is the center of the islands' musical and theatrical activities

Some of Bermuda's trees, adapted to a semitropical climate, resemble giant cacti

Also found on the Harrington Sound road is the North Nature Reserve, containing many birds, flowers, and trees. The Reserve also contains a mangrove forest, which is not quite land and not quite sea. The floor of the forest is flooded at high tide and muddy at low tide, and the mangrove roots are visible above ground. Home to many unusual animals, mangrove trees drop their spearlike seeds into the mud near their roots. Although they flourish here, mangroves have all but vanished from most other areas of Bermuda.

Another wildlife sanctuary, the 60-acre Spittal Pond, is located in Smith's. It is home to more than 25 types of birds.

A diver confronts a small shark at the aquarium in Flatts Inlet

More than 100 varieties of sea life are housed in the aquarium

Visitors to the aquarium can listen to a recorded "tour" of the exhibits

Construction began in 1874, but this church in St. George's was never completed; instead, funds were used to build two other churches

Hamilton Parish

Hamilton Parish covers the northern and eastern shores of Harrington Sound. It is bordered on the north by the Atlantic, on the east by Castle Harbour, and on the west by Flatts Inlet.

Bermuda's aquarium, which houses 100 types of local sea animals and a wide variety of species from around the world, is located at Flatts Inlet. At Church Bay, also on Harrington Sound, is one of the island's oldest churches—Holy Trinity Church, which was built in 1623.

Many pottery and perfume factories are located in Hamilton Parish; the perfumes are made from locally grown lilies and passion flowers.

One special feature of Hamilton Parish is the number and variety of its caves. Dozens of caves, both above and under water, have been explored.

Traditional white limestone architecture is illustrated in this farmhouse in Smith's Parish

St. George's Parish

Home of Bermuda's original capital, the town of St. George's, St. George's Parish is bordered on three sides by the Atlantic Ocean. On its southern side, the parish faces Castle Harbour. The parish is essentially a group of islands encompassed by a coral reef—the very section of reef which, 350 years ago, caused the wreck of the *Sea Venture*.

The town of St. George's looks much the same today as when it was the capital. Still standing are many of the original homes, the town hall, the old State House, the footpaths, and even the stocks where people were publicly punished for civil crimes during the 17th century.

The Severn Bridge connects St. George's Island with St. David's Island. St. David's was once three separate islands called Longbird, St. David's, and Cooper's. They were filled in and made into one large island by the United States government in 1941. Today, a United States naval air station is located on St. David's.

Tucker's Town, an isolated part of St. George's Parish, is south of Castle Harbour beside Hamilton Parish. For centuries a fishing and whaling town, Tucker's Town became a wealthy resort in the 1920s. Near Tucker's Town are Bermuda's famous "natural arches," huge rock archways carved by the continual pounding of the surf against the caves on the shore.

Somers Wharf is a popular shopping area for Bermuda's tourists

Stone buildings erected in the 17th century by British settlers still stand on Castle Island

The People and Society

They came to Bermuda in various ways; they endured hardships, developed cultures, and lived in varying economic conditions. The people of Bermuda, struggling with their islands' problems and sometimes struggling with each other, are remarkably diverse.

Bermuda's population now numbers approximately 55,000. Of these, about 60 percent are black, 10 percent are of Portuguese descent, and the rest are of various ethnic origins. There is a large white population of British descent. A brief look at how their ancestors came to Bermuda and at some of the events that have shaped their history makes the people of present-day Bermuda easier to understand.

Bermuda's British heritage is seen in the islands' flag, which has a Union Jack in the top left corner; to the right is the Bermudian coat of arms

A Struggle for Political Equality

During the period when Bermuda's whites were striving to become a colony, they also longed to live in the same grand plantation style as England's other colonies, particularly Virginia. To live on a plantation required many things: the most important was the slave.

Powerful emotions are stirred by the word "slave"—visions of cruel punishments, of families heartlessly torn apart, of a life without freedom, and of grueling, thankless work. But colonists felt that slaves were the missing ingredient needed to complete the style of plantation life in Bermuda.

Not all slaves were black people. In addition to Africans, the colonists of Bermuda bought and sold American Indians who had caused trouble for the British on the mainland, in Virginia and other colonies. Also, some slaves were of Irish and Scottish descent, enslaved because they were politically opposed to Britain's ruthless and powerful prime minister, Oliver Cromwell.

The African slaves, most of whom arrived on the islands from other English colonies, made several attempts—over a period of 200 years—to gain freedom. When Bermuda's 4,000 slaves were freed in 1834, they constituted 50 percent of Bermuda's population. The blacks in Bermuda have continued to fight a steady uphill battle for equality. Like American blacks, they have met resistance almost every step of the way.

The year 1959 was a turning point for Bermudian society and a time of change for its black people. In celebration of the 350th anniversary of the *Sea Venture* wreck, two plays—*This Island's*

Built in 1892, the governor's mansion has 62 rooms

Mine and *My Heart Stays Here*—were performed. Using the emotionally uplifting themes of these plays as a catalyst, young black leaders like Dr. Stanley Ratteray seized the chance to lead their people toward equality. Ratteray engineered successful boycotts in an effort to desegregate the movie theaters of Bermuda. The boycotts worked so well that after only two weeks black people were attending movies and plays with whites.

The successful desegregation of the movie theaters led to other changes. Hotels and restaurants were desegregated. White-owned businesses, formerly employing only whites behind their counters, began to hire blacks.

Because of the islands' warm temperatures, short pants are an option in school uniforms

During this period, a black man, W.L. Tucker, was appointed to Bermuda's Executive Council. He was the first black council member. In 1960, Tucker's committee initiated what was eventually to become a dramatic revision of Bermuda's voting laws. Up to that time, landowners could vote in every parish in which they held land. An individual who had real estate in four different parishes, for example, could vote in all four parishes. But while landowners had great power in the electoral process, people who had no land holdings (who leased or rented their homes) could not vote at all. Tucker insisted that it was not right for people to be able to vote in more than one parish. He also asserted that people who did not own land should still have the right to vote. In 1963, a franchise bill became law. It entitled every adult over age 25 to one vote, while landowners were given only one extra vote. Although the wealthy continued to hold an obvious advantage at the ballot box, important progress toward democratic elections had been made.

St. David's Island was once three separate islands

Blacks rapidly began to win political office. With the birth of the Progressive Labour Party and its immediate successor, the United Bermuda Party, the black majority soon gained control over the House of Assembly. The United Bermuda Party radically changed the entire direction of political life on the islands. They used their control of the House to change the "plus one" voting law, giving each citizen over age 21 one—and only one—vote. They also decided to rewrite the entire constitution and start a cabinet system of government.

Throughout much of this period of dramatic change, white banker Sir Henry Tucker helped control the flow of government. When Tucker stepped down as government leader in 1971, Bermudians witnessed a substantial sign of change: his successor was Sir Edward Richards—a black man.

Social Separation

As much as any of Britain's other colonies, Bermuda has a deeply rooted tie to the Queen, to aristocracy, and to the pomp and circumstance connected with royalty. At the forefront of Bermuda's own white aristocracy are families descended from the islands' first white settlers. Known by those who oppose them as the "Forty Thieves" families, they are symbols of the difficulties that Bermuda's blacks have faced.

The Forty Thieves families held political and economic control of Bermuda for more than two centuries. They have been accused of manipulating Parliament, controlling elections, and running the financial life of the islands in their own best interests.

The Mid Ocean Golf Club in Tucker's Town, one of many courses

Although most political powers have shifted in recent years from the wealthy white minority to the working-class black majority, social distinctions persist between the races and classes in Bermuda.

For many years, wealthy Bermudians have belonged to exclusive tennis, golf, civic, social, and literary clubs. The Forty Thieves families founded many of these clubs, all of which banned black people from membership. Portuguese, poor white people, and various other nationalities were also refused membership in the exclusive clubs. These discriminatory practices had far-reaching implications for Bermudian society. The people excluded from the well-to-do white clubs operated their own clubs. Thus, the initial exclusion of blacks by the Forty Thieves clubs has been instrumental in segregating the races of Bermuda.

Art Forms

The people of Bermuda have developed two original forms of art unique to the islands: a special style of architecture and Gombey dancing.

Bermuda's weather and its building-block limestone greatly affected the direction taken by Bermudian architecture. Because the stone is abundant, it has been used more than any other construction material. At first, the architects designed flat roofs, but they absorbed too much water from the frequent rains; the steep roof was found to be more effective.

The steep roofs led to shorter walls, and many doors are as high as the ceilings inside the houses. Homes were also designed

An unpaved driveway leads to a cottage on the scenic South Shore

with basements for housing slaves. The so-called "welcoming arms" staircases that led down to these basements flared broadly at their bases.

Another aspect of Bermudian architecture exists because of the shortage of fresh water. Rainwater, after running off of the steep roofs, is directed toward storage tanks. These tanks are still used for a variety of things, including bathing.

From the 17th through the 19th centuries, fireplaces were for cooking, so traditional Bermudian architecture had to include chimneys. The summers in Bermuda are long and hot, and no one wanted to increase the heat. The distinctive feature of the Bermuda chimney, therefore, is that it is located outside the house. It has a broad base with an opening that can be used from inside the house if needed. Many of the wealthiest people had kitchens entirely separate from the rest of their houses, the technique employed on Virginia plantations.

Hurricanes also influenced architects' designs. Windows were made small and thick, with window blinds of sturdy wood, for protection from wind and driving rain. Cedar was the most abundant wood, but trees longer than 15 or 20 feet (4 or 6 meters) were hard to find. The 15-foot trees used as beams accounted for the narrowness of the houses.

A traditional island cottage now houses the St. George's Historical Society

Island artisans create pottery and other wares for sale to tourists

The 18th-century homes were more specifically Bermudian than those designed later, because architects of the 19th and 20th centuries were influenced by other cultures. In the 19th century, for example, Victorian architecture was introduced to the islands. Since World War II, architects have designed both modern and 18th-century-style buildings in Bermuda. Many of them use the traditional lime wash as paint.

Bermuda has a cultural tradition—an art form—that expresses the lore, the social mores, and the musical heritage of its African people. It is called "Gombey."

A mixture of African, West Indian, British, and American Indian influences, Gombey is a traditional dance performed on the day after Christmas. The dancers dress in ornate costumes, including brilliantly colored headdressses covered with mirrors. Children and adults separate into groups, dancing rhythmically—sometimes feverishly—to the steady beat of drums and other percussion instruments. Today, Gombey dancing can be seen throughout the year in a variety of places on the islands.

Gombey dancing highlights Bermuda's Christmas celebration

A young Bermudian in the ornate attire of a Gombey dancer

The Mahicans

A special group of Bermudians, the Mahicans, live on St. David's Island. They are distinctive-looking, with features like those of American Indians. The Mahicans were brought to Bermuda as slaves in the 1600s from New York. The Mahicans reportedly resent being called Bermudians—they think of St. David's Island as their home and are not interested in the rest of Bermuda. Nor do they follow British tradition. A Mahican cricket match, for example, will include very loud yelling and heavy betting—things not done in England or in other parts of the Bermuda islands.

63

One of the favorite foods of the Mahicans is spiced shark meat. They are expert fishermen, especially knowledgeable about the reef around St. David's. Through the centuries, they have piloted ships through the coral. Tales tell of Mahican crews, their bronzed arms glistening in the sun, fiercely rowing more than 100 miles (160 kilometers) in a single trip.

The Mahican pilots made their best living during the Civil War in the United States. England wanted the South's cotton, and Bermuda was chosen as the stopover spot. The Mahicans became perhaps the best blockade-runners of all.

Fort St. Catherine, a 19th-century fortress, is a well-known landmark in Hamilton

People and Their Environment

As in many parts of the world, a great dilemma now faces Bermuda: how much building and growth can the country tolerate without destroying its natural environment? With the rise in service industries and housing that has accompanied the increased tourist boom in recent decades, many Bermudians fear that some things that give their country character—the forests of cedar and palmettos, the marshes, the pockets of wilderness—are being eroded. The very qualities that attract visitors to this island wonderland are in danger of extinction.

Bermuda's history is evident even on its beaches, which are lined with ancient seawalls

But Bermudians are taking steps to ensure the survival of the natural wilderness areas and to recapture much of the native character of their islands.

In the year 1500, experts estimate, more than a million cahow birds lived on the islands. The early settlers and their descendants ate the cahows and their eggs. In fact, the settlers nearly ate the cahow bird into extinction. Only after the discovery in 1951 of a small nesting colony of cahows on an offshore island did Bermudians realize that the species still survived. Bermuda has made the entire Castle Harbour island group a bird sanctuary. With help from the country's Department of Agriculture and Fisheries—and other organizations such as the New York Zoological Society—the ancient bird of Bermuda whose cries greeted the first seafarers centuries ago has a good chance of increasing its tiny population.

Other efforts are under way to conserve Bermuda's environment. Stokes Point Nature Reserve, a two-acre marsh, was once filled with garbage. Purchased by the Audubon Society, it is now being restored to its original state. At Nonsuch, a 14-acre island in the Castle Harbour group, Bermuda is hoping to create a living outdoor museum of native plants and to build a predator-free environment for rare and endangered animals.

The people of Bermuda are wrestling with a delicate but vital issue of the 20th century: how to allow growth without destroying the native riches of the islands. Bermudians are determined to find a way in which the cahow bird and the sunbather can thrive together.

Although pineapple trees and other fruits grow on the islands, Bermuda does not export produce

Of Many Faiths

In the venerable city of St. George's stands a building that breathes history—St. Peter's Church. In the early 1600s, a wooden church stood on this site. The present stone church was erected in 1713 and is the oldest continuously used Protestant church in the western hemisphere. The aroma of centuries-old cedar from its beams and rafters fills the sanctuary. Inside stand the altar, built in 1624; an ironstone baptismal font, believed to be of 15th-century origin; and a silver communion service, a gift from King William III of England and his wife, Mary II. The church's walls are lined with memorials to the historic figures of Bermuda.

The churches of many cities and towns in Bermuda are guides to the past. The musty relics and graveyard inscriptions tell ancient stories of the first settlers. In religious matters, as in many other areas of life, Bermuda somewhat mirrors Great Britain. Although freedom of religion is now scrupulously respected in the islands, the Church of England has always been important in Bermudian society. The Anglican Bishop commands a place of eminence much like that enjoyed by the Archbishop of Canterbury.

In the Anglican Cathedral of the Most Holy Trinity, in Hamilton, the Bishop of Bermuda presides among stained-glass win-

The Cathedral of the Most Holy Trinity in Hamilton

The wooden altar of old St. Peter's Church dates from 1624

dows, British oak sculpture, hand-embroidered prayer cushions, and throne-chairs for visiting royalty and other dignitaries. The church's Gothic tower dominates the Hamilton skyline, much as the Anglican Church has dominated the religious life of the islands.

From the earliest days of the colony, however, other religious denominations have built churches. The Presbyterian Church of Scotland, Christ Church, claims to have had a congregation in Bermuda since 1612. Its church in Warwick, which still stands today,

71

was built in 1719 and is one of the island's oldest.

In March of 1748, the famous Methodist preacher George Whitefield visited Bermuda. He stayed for two months, wandering around the islands and generally giving two sermons every day. Half a century later, another Methodist made the trek to Bermuda from America. The Reverend John Stephenson arrived determined to preach the gospel to the "Black and Coloured people," as other Methodist preachers had begun to do in other parts of the world. Stephenson was soon arrested for breaking a law prohibiting "pretending" ministers from preaching the gospel. White Bermudians were not yet ready for black churches.

But in 1825, Chief Justice John Christie Esten—a man with more advanced opinions on the race question—offered land at Cobb's Hill where a chapel for slaves could be constructed. The work was quickly undertaken by Edward Frazer, a slave, who exhorted the black people of Warwick to work on the chapel. On moonlit nights and holidays, whenever the slaves could get free time from their labors, men, women, and children hauled stone from nearby quarries to the site. The job took two years. The church is still standing.

Other black churches also appeared, most built by slaves. Across from the imposing Anglican Cathedral in Hamilton stands St. Paul's African Methodist Episcopal Church. One of the island's most prestigious black churches, St. Paul's was erected in 1881 and, like the other black churches built in the 19th century, is a testament to the determination of Bermuda's black citizens to establish a solid religious community.

The Church of St. Mark in Smith's Parish

Throughout Bermuda's early history, the dominance of the Anglican Church made the establishment of the Catholic Church impossible on the islands. By the 1840s, however, Catholic priests began to visit Bermuda, mainly to see Catholic soldiers stationed there, to visit convicts in prisons, and to conduct religious services for the few Catholic residents. By the second half of the 19th century, the Portuguese families arriving in Bermuda had greatly increased the Catholic population. During the early 20th century, a number of Catholic churches began to appear. Today, the Catholic Church in Bermuda is active and vigorous.

The islands of Bermuda are inhabited by men and women of many different religious groups. There are Baptists, members of the Church of Jesus Christ of Latter-Day Saints (Mormons), Christian Scientists, Jehovah's Witnesses, Lutherans, Seventh Day Adventists, and members of the Church of the Nazarene, the Church of Christ, and the Church of God. For these and others, Bermuda's religious life is rich, another sign of the diversity of its people and institutions.

The turquoise water of the western Atlantic encircles Castle Island

Sessions Houses, where the islands' governing body meets, was built in the early 1800s; the clock spire, called Jubilee Tower, commemorates the 50th anniversary of Queen Victoria's coronation

Government: In the British Image

Bermuda is Britain's oldest colony, and many of its institutions are very much like those of Britain. Its government is a good example; it closely resembles that of the United Kingdom. The country is self-governing, with a parliamentary system. The governor is appointed by the Queen of England and represents the Crown's interests in the islands. The governor's title is "His Excellency the Governor and Commander-in-Chief of the Bermuda or Somers Islands." He is responsible for police matters, national defense, and relations with foreign countries.

The Bermuda Parliament has two houses: the Senate, similar to the British House of Lords, is the upper house; the House of Assembly is the lower house. The Cabinet, led by the premier, forms the executive branch of government and represents the party in power, much as the prime minister does in England.

The House of Assembly is composed of 40 members chosen from 20 electoral districts. For actions taken by the Assembly to become law, they must be approved by the Senate. The Senate is composed of 11 members, some appointed on the advice of the premier, others on the recommendation of the governor and the leader of the opposition party.

The legal system in Bermuda has also been modeled closely after the British legal system, with justices of the peace, justices of the Court of the King's Bench, and Masters of the Court of Chancery. Under the Constitution of 1968, appointments to the judiciary are the direct responsibility of the Governor. The Judicial Department itself is headed by the Chief Justice, who presides over the Supreme Court. Visitors to Bermuda today see court officials wearing the black robes and powdered wigs that are so much a part of Britain's legal history.

The constitution contains a Bill of Rights, similar in tone and spirit to the English Magna Carta and the American Bill of Rights, that protects basic freedoms and liberties.

Bermuda's self-defense force, the Bermuda Regiment, is 450 soldiers strong; Her Royal Highness Princess Margaret is its Commander-in-Chief

Several military bases are located in Bermuda. The United States maintains a naval air station at Kindley Field and operates another installation in Southampton. Land for these stations was a gift from Bermuda to the United States during World War II.

Bermuda has had a long-standing military connection with Britain. As early as 1797, the British Royal Navy had established a base on the islands. After a residence of almost 200 years, the British Army garrison was withdrawn in 1957. The Bermuda Regiment, with a strength of approximately 450 part-time soldiers, is Bermuda's own self-defense force. Her Royal Highness Princess Margaret presented the colors to the Regiment in 1965 and in 1984 was made its Commander-in-Chief.

The islands' government has undertaken various social security programs. Mostly dating from the mid-1960s, they include old age, disability, and survivor pensions and hospitalization insurance for all citizens.

Since the heroic days of the hardy 17th-century adventurers, Bermuda has come a long way toward establishing and maintaining a stable government. And although talk of independence stirs strong emotions in Bermuda today, the government of the islands—like its history—remains thoroughly British in origin and character.

A Sports Lover's Haven

Bermuda is one of the world's most popular island resorts. The weather is gentle, the pace of life relaxing, the scenery alternately breathtaking and tranquil. Sports and recreational activities are numerous and varied.

Although some visitors to Bermuda choose reflective, even sedentary, activities, many seek more active pursuits. From a pensive stroll down one of the many flower-lined roads or paths to an encounter with a shark, life in Bermuda can take almost any direction.

The wooden sloop **Chicane** *can be chartered by visitors to Hamilton Harbour*

Sir Brownlow Gray built Bermuda's first tennis courts in 1873

Bermuda's uncrowded pink beaches seem to stretch forever; they offer ideal sunbathing and swimming. For tourists with a more adventurous spirit, the coral reefs on all sides of the islands provide a rich environment in which to snorkel or scuba dive. Thousands of brilliantly colored fish, darting in unison, seem constantly wary as they travel their reef; the barracuda cuts like a knife through the water. The coral is the center of this ecosystem—without it none of the other life would thrive. Some coral is shaped like oversized brains; other corals look like delicate blue fans, gently swaying to the rhythm of the sea.

Water sports such as skiing, sailing and windsurfing are immensely popular with natives and visitors alike. The huge lake of Harrington Sound is one of the best areas for boating, and Great

Cricket, a popular sport in Britain, is also a tradition in Bermuda; here, hundreds of spectators watch a Cup Match

Every spring, the annual Kite Festival is held at Horseshoe Bay

83

Bermuda's many shoals and reefs are ideal for snorkeling

Sound is also heavily traveled by all types of pleasure craft. One of the world's most popular yachting centers, Bermuda is home to the International One Design World Championships, which attract entries from all over the world.

Fishing is both the livelihood of many Bermudians and the year-round sport of visitors. Fishermen pursue dolphin, tuna, albacore, barracuda, white marlin, wahoo, and bonito in the deep waters outside the coral reef. Gray and yellowtail snapper, a smaller version of the barracuda, rockfish, pompano, and bonefish are caught inside or near the reef. Although some people believe barracuda to be poisonous, it is edible, and the islanders find it especially tasty when deep-fried. Fishing brings certain risks, however. Four-hundred-pound tiger sharks, eight feet in length, have on occasion injured unlucky fishermen.

The Annual Game Fishing Tournament runs from May through November each year. On May 1st, the islands' charter boats assemble for the Tournament Fleet Parade, which makes its way from Hamilton Harbour to the open sea and officially opens the fishing season.

Jogging has become popular all over the world and Bermuda is no exception. Native Bermudians participate daily in group runs, and visitors are welcome to join. The island also sponsors an internationally competitive 10-kilometer (six-mile) race and a marathon (26.2 miles; 42 kilometers) every January.

Golf has increased in popularity on the islands in recent years, just as in the United States. The Bermuda Golf Association sponsors 13 annual tournaments, most of which are played between November and February. Bermuda's eight golf courses offer a variety suited to the needs and skills of any golfer. At least three of these courses are of championship caliber.

Sir Brownlow Gray built the island's first tennis court in Paget Parish in 1873. The sport was played there by a young lady named Mary Outerbridge, who introduced tennis to the United States in 1874. The sport is still played on more than 100 courts in Bermuda today. As in the United States, tennis in Bermuda is no longer a sport solely of the upper classes; everyone can play. The climate allows tennis lovers to play year-round, and the Coral Beach tournaments for juniors and adults take place every winter.

Several spectator sports are popular in Bermuda, but none more so than the weekly cricket matches held on Sundays from May to September. After the cricket season ends in the fall, rugby is played until Christmas. The soccer season is longer, starting in October and running through April. Sailboat races also occur on Sundays in Harrington Sound, and motorboat races are held during the summer and fall in St. George's Parish.

From the sailor to the golfer, from the beachcomber to the fisherman, from the tennis player to the jogger, Bermuda is a sports lover's paradise.

Sport fishermen display their catch at Devonshire Dock

A Tourist Economy

The time-worn skeletons of Spanish and British ships on the ocean floor around Bermuda tell the story of a country whose destiny has been born and shaped by the sea. Mariners who sailed the Atlantic trade routes knew the menace of its uncharted turquoise waters. But, because of the fortitude of those early sailors, the country grew and prospered. Its development and fortune were made possible by the sea and the industries and activities to which it gave life: whaling, ship-building, trading, and privateering. Bermudians made their mark in the world with their seafaring exploits.

Today, the people of Bermuda enjoy a high standard of living. There is no national debt and almost no unemployment. But Bermuda's prosperity no longer depends on its marine activities.

Colorful flags fly from the masts of pleasure craft moored in one of Bermuda's many harbors

Fishing has long been an important industry in Bermuda; this turn-of-the-century photograph shows commercial fishermen preparing for work

Bermuda has no mining industry. The islands do export some goods—perfume, pharmaceutical products, and liqueurs. The islands are also known for their magnificent lilies, hardy and fragrant, which were first brought to Bermuda in the 19th century from the Liukiu Islands in Japan. The Bermuda Lily is now perhaps the islands' best-known export, recognized as *the* Easter lily in much of the United States.

But although the country yields rich flowers, fruits and vegetables (including its famous onions), its economy has turned to tourism. The story persists that tourism as a significant national industry had its origins with the visit of Princess Louise, daughter of Queen Victoria, in the early 1880s. Princess Louise had fled to Bermuda to escape the bitter winter of Canada, where her husband was governor-general. Her visit led to the opening of the magnificent Princess Hotel in Hamilton. The elegant style of the hotel set a trend for many later resorts.

In the late 1800s, the wealthy began to flock to Bermuda with their maids, their trunks full of expensive clothes, and their tennis rackets. They roamed the islands in carriages, played in tennis tournaments, and sipped tea in luxurious spots along the coast. Soon, a suntan was a status symbol.

In the 1920s air flights were available, and steamships made weekly crossings to the islands. Bermuda became a resort haven. Visitors began to arrive not only in the winter but year-round, filling cottages and hotels and exploring the islands' less accessible areas. A charming (if sometimes undependable) railway was constructed between Hamilton and St. George's.

The tourist industry now accounts for a larger share of the country's economy than all other industries combined. More than 100 resorts are scattered across the islands. Luxurious hotels and apartments, guest houses and yacht clubs, fine restaurants, beauti-

A visit to the Maritime Museum is a voyage into Bermuda's seafaring past

ful golf courses, snorkeling expeditions for experts and amateurs, tennis courts, and lush gardens entice the visitor. Most attractive of all, however, is the wondrous natural grandeur of Bermuda: the shore itself, from the craggy Spanish Rock area to Church Bay and beyond. Over the centuries, the fierce drumming of the Atlantic, carving rugged cliffs and jutting inlets, has created a beachcomber's and sunbather's heaven.

Every day, cruise ships leave harbors in St. George's and Hamilton to tour the reef and coastal rocks that were so dreaded by sailors centuries ago and are so admired by visitors today. Bicycles and mopeds carry eager tourists through the islands. More adventuresome tourists explore the nearby waters, some even hiring veteran seamen to dive for the wrecks of Spanish galleons.

Tourism is controlled by the government. Limits have been placed on the building of new hotels owned by non-Bermudians. Charter flights and cruise ships can dock only at certain times. Laws also restrict the number, size, and horsepower of automobiles. Although Woodrow Wilson would be disappointed that automobiles are allowed on Bermuda at all (he supported a permanent ban), he would probably applaud these restrictions.

More than half a million tourists now flock to the islands each year, bringing an estimated 356 million dollars in income to Bermuda. Most of the tourism revenue is in United States dollars: 88 percent of the visitors are American. Approximately 5 percent are Canadian and the rest are from Britain and elsewhere. Sixty-five cents of each dollar spent in Bermuda comes from the tourist industry.

In addition to tourism, the islands have many insurance companies and other financial institutions. In order to lure some light industry, Bermuda has offered tax advantages to companies; a number of firms have moved to the islands in recent years. The country also enjoys revenues from the United States military personnel stationed there. In the 1960s, as Americans launched their new space exploration program, the U.S. National Aeronautics and Space Administration (NASA) selected Bermuda as one of the sites for a tracking station. The Bermuda station gave important support to the Apollo moon-landing program.

Tourists come to Bermuda for its beaches and its history

The city of Hamilton is not only the seat of government but the capital of business. Businessmen zip along its busy streets on mopeds. Their typical business suit consists of a coat and tie, knee socks, and Bermuda shorts. The department stores and shops lining Hamilton's main streets carry items imported from Europe: linens from Ireland, teacups from England, sweaters from Scotland, watches from Switzerland, perfumes from France.

Bermuda's tourist economy is robust. And as long as the winds and tides of the coast whip white surf against the cliffs and the tropical breezes blow warm, Bermuda will probably remain a prosperous center of tourism.

The rose-colored coral of Bermuda that gives the sand its pinkish cast has known the footsteps of many people. English settlers watched the near extinction of the cahow bird without concern; their descendants now fight for the bird's survival. The Portuguese workers helped cut down the cedar groves; their descendants now plant new groves. The Africans, forced upon the shores, lifted the limestone blocks for the island homes; their descendants in government now help determine the laws and codes for those homes.

The islands of Bermuda are relatively small; the entire population is roughly that of a small American city. But the people of the islands are as diverse and rich in heritage as can be found anywhere. They have had struggles, disappointments, and triumphs. They have made mistakes. And, for people everywhere, life has meant learning from those mistakes and attempting to change and grow. The people have learned and changed. Bermuda has grown.

Index

airlines 27–28, 89
American Civil War 23–24, 64
American Revolution 21–22
Anglican (see Church of England)
Annual Game Fishing Tournament 85
Apollo space program 91
archipelago 34
architecture 58–59
art 58
Audubon Society 67
automobiles 26

Baptists 74
barracuda 82
Bermuda Volunteer Rifle Corps 27
Bermuda coral 32
Bermuda Regiment 80
"Bermuda chimney" 60
Bermuda Company 15
Bermuda Lily 88
Bermuda Golf Association 85
Bermudez, Juan de 14, 34
Bill of Rights 79
Bishop of Bermuda 69
blockade running 24

Boaz Island 36
"Boilers" 37
Botanical Garden 38
British Royal Navy 27, 28, 80

Cabinet Building 39
cahow bird 9, 66, 68, 92
Cape Hatteras, North Carolina 8
Castle Harbour 47, 67
Cathedral of the Most Holy Trinity 39, 69
caves 47
cedar trees 12, 19, 38, 60, 65
Christ Church 71
Christian Scientists 74
Church Bay 37, 47, 90
Church of Christ 74
Church of England 69–71
Church of God 74
Church of Jesus Christ of Latter-Day Saints (Mormons) 74
Church of the Nazarene 74
City Hall 39
climate 32–33
Cobb's Hill 72
Cobbler's Island 39

coins 18
Cooper's Island 49
Coral Beach Club tennis
 tournament 86
coral 34, 82, 92
Court of Chancery 78
Court of the King's Bench 78
cricket 63, 86
Cromwell, Oliver 52
currency 18

Department of Agriculture and
 Fisheries 67
Devil's Hole Pond 43
Devonshire Marsh 40
Devonshire Parish 40–43

Esten, John Christie (Chief Justice)
 72
Executive Council 54

fireplaces 59–60
fish 85
fishing 64, 85
Flatts Inlet 47
Flatts Village 43
Fort Hamilton 40
"Forty Thieves" families 56–58
Frazer, Edward 72

Gates, Sir Thomas 9
Gates Fort 16
Gibbs Hill 37
golf 85–86, 90
Gombey dancing 58, 62

Government House 29
governor 77
Grape Bay 38
Gray, Sir Brownlow 86
Great Sound 82–85
Gulf Stream 22

Hamilton (city) 22, 25, 38, 92
Hamilton Harbour 38, 85
Hamilton Parish 47, 90
Happy Valley Road 40
Harrington Sound 43, 47, 82, 86
Harvey, Cpt. Darrell 20
"Hog Money" 18
Horseshoe Bay 37
House of Assembly 56, 77
Hungry Bay 38
hurricanes 60

independence 29
Ireland Islands 36–37
"Isle of Devils" 8, 12

Jehovah's Witnesses 74
Jobson's Cove 38
Jordan, Silvanus 12
Judicial Department 78

Kindley Field 80
King, Martin Luther, Jr. 29

"La Bermuda" 14
lilies 47
limestone 21, 32, 39, 58, 92
Longbird Island 49

Louise, Princess 88
Lutherans 74

Mahicans 63
mangroves 38, 44
Margaret, Princess 80
Mary Celestia 24
military bases 80
Moore, Richard 12
Mormons (see Church of Jesus Christ of Latter-Day Saints)
My Heart Stays Here 53

National Aeronautics and Space Administration (NASA) 91
natural arches 31
New York Zoological Society 67
Newport, Cpt. Christopher 9
Nonsuch 67
North Nature Reserve 44

oleander 43
"Onion Town" 25
onions 24–25
oranges 19
Outerbridge, Mary 86

Paget marsh 38
Paget Parish 38, 86
palmetto trees 12, 38, 65
Parliament 16, 56, 77
Parliament Street 39
Pembroke Parish 38–40
perfume 47
pirates 20–21

Plough 12
population 51
Portuguese 22–23, 51, 58, 74, 92
Presbyterian Church of Scotland (see Christ Church)
Princess Hotel 28, 88
Progressive Labour Party 29, 56
Prohibition 27

"Quo Fata Ferunt" 29

R.E. Lee 23–24
race riots 29
Ratteray, Dr. Stanley 53
reefs 8, 34, 48, 82
Richards, Sir Edward 56
"Roaring Twenties" 27
Roman Catholic Church 74
rugby 86

Sandys Parish 36–37
scuba diving 82
Sea Venture 9–12, 14, 15, 48, 52
Senate 77
Sessions House 39
Seventh Day Adventists 74
Severn Bridge 49
Shakespeare, William 9
shark meat 64
Sharples, Sir Richard 29
slaves 16, 52
Smith's Parish 43–44
snorkeling 82, 90
Somers, Sir George 9, 12
Somerset Island 36

Southampton Parish 37
Spanish Rock 90
Spittal Pond 44
St. Catherine 16
St. Paul's African Methodist
  Episcopal Church 72
St. Peter's Church 16, 69
St. George's Parish 16, 48–49, 86, 90
St. George's (city) 15, 22, 49
St. David's Island 49, 63
State House 16
Stephenson, Rev. John 72
Stokes Point Nature Reserve 67
Stonehole Bay 37
Sugar Cane Point 37
Supreme Court 79

Tempest, The 9
This Island's Mine 52–53
tourism 25–26, 65, 90–92
Tournament Fleet parade 85

treasure 34–35
Tucker, Sir Henry 56
Tucker, W. L. 54–55
Tucker's Town 49
Twain, Mark 25, 29

United Bermuda Party 56

Warwick Camp 38
Warwick Long Bay 38
Warwick, Second Earl of 38
Warwick Parish 38
Washington, Gen. George 21
Watford Bridge 37
Wellington, Duke of 40
whaling 19, 87
Whitefield, George 72
Wilson, Woodrow 26, 90
windsurfing 82
witch hunts 18–19
World War I 26–27
World War II 28, 61, 80